Dirty Laundry

Dirty Laundry

Deborah Alma

Nine
Arches
Press

Dirty Laundry
Deborah Alma

ISBN: 9781911027416

First published May 2018 by:

Nine Arches Press
Unit 14, Sir Frank Whittle Business Centre,
Great Central Way, Rugby.
CV21 3XH
United Kingdom

www.ninearchespress.com

Printed in the United Kingdom by:
Imprint Digital

Nine Arches Press is supported using public funding through Arts Council England.

Supported using public funding by
**ARTS COUNCIL
ENGLAND**

For Geoffrey Alma and Rubina Alma-Claxton with love

CONTENTS

Flock

i.m. of Jo Cox

Three chickens died this week.
They sat in the unexpected heat panting
and in the morning there was just one
white bird, bewildered, stepping over
their bodies, following the dog.

In the news, a woman died
and for days the rain,
so that the roses rotted in the bud

and there seemed, in all this time
of high summer and scent,
of hollyhocks and hedge-clippings,
that I had had enough

and finding black feathers
floating on the pond
was too much.

Morning Song

An open-windowed church-belled morning
chimes of loss and mine; water pipes sing,

and I bring back to bed a blue enamel
pot of hot coffee, as silk as the slide

of skin on sheets, and rough hot bread
warmed in an oven kept in overnight

and bite into a grape and lazy eyed
the women I have been no longer fight their corners;

cocks-crow, black throats thrown back with old songs,
flown back to all of these edges of me,

they stay and stare, these women, across the hazy
sun-strewn wooden floor of my dreams

and my ageing; the mirror crazed
and hung with beads, the pink and the red

and the purple of the stocks I have grown
and the white of the daisies.

One Mother

Cheryl can't stand it any longer,
the ewes calling for the lambs.

All day was bad enough, but moving
on the edges of sleep, she counts the bleats,

frantic, the milk twitching at teats.
She can feel it, needing the pull and pull,

the milk's steady pulse beating,
mild woolly agony on and on, until

almost silent, one mother – it would be her –
never giving up, running back and forth

through the hedge gap; searching,
wild as a wolf howling for the moon.

The double glazing cannot shut it out.
Thin-skinned and comfortable

in council estate concrete,
Cheryl turns her face from the moles'

fly-blown purses strung along the fence,
tells him she wants to go home.

Nearly Love

I nearly fell in love once.
He came round and found the list on the fridge,
leant over to read it carefully, winked,
picked up a pencil, and ticked and ticked
and ticked all the boxes.

After I told him it wasn't working,
my friends and family, astonished,
pointed to the list. But I said,

I will not drink from the cup
that comes up in small tiptoes
and black shoes, that sits
at the end of the bed, waiting;
its mouth an oh *of ordinary;*
comfort and safety and sex;
a drug of slowing, of rest, like death
already come.

They could not see this.
They knew what was best.

Borderline

Do you walk on eggshells asked the therapist?
No! I crunch through them
in my Dr. Marten boots,
bashing in their little skulls,
breaking the beaks
that tap and pip, scratching for the light,
scrambling blood and sensitive bone.
Good! he said.

Do you eat the shells of eggs asked the terrapin?
No! I munch through them,
using red claws and truths,
spitting out the grit from the blood
but when I get to the heart,
though it cannot be broken and is not mine,
I am gentle and leave it alone.
Good! he said.

Will you unscramble my secrets asked the terrorist?
Love me after the cracks,
the big fall, prop up the wall,
and protect me from the hooves of the horses,
the bayonets of the men?
Put me together again and again?
No! I said.

Then in June

The cuckoo comes in April,
sings a song in May,
then in June another tune
and then he flies away...
English folklore, 1869 (Hazlitt)

The cuckoo does not know itself to be a cuckoo
and is to be pitied. It cracks its own egg
and pushes out its bloodied head,
opening and shutting its beak
just like the tiny others.
Sweetheart, I say, *Just move over,*
you're stopping their breaths.

I cannot stand it
and so, in my own kind of pain,
push the big baby over the edge,
see it fall on the concrete,
see in the blood spreading out
that it is still alive.
But I have worms to catch
and other fish to fry.

Cattle Lorry Lover

You meet me in the lay-by
on the A49. Is it my heart
or the restlessness of the c
stomping and steaming p

You kiss my breasts,
sucking at the nipples,
whilst calves from their mothers
are forced to wait

for my breathing to calm.
Their eyes startle and I climb down,
get back into my Volvo estate.
They sway away
and my breasts' milk drips.

I Am My Own Parent

I love my red shoes,
all of the shoes I have loved,
they are.

I swing my legs against the wall,
scuffing them slightly.
My Dad is not here to pick them up

by the scruffs of their dirty necks
and leave them shining in the morning.
Instead, the arc of my swing

not quite so high,
the shoes every day a little duller.
At night I leave them in the hall like hope.

In the morning,
absentmindedly dreaming of old loves
and reading poetry until it hurts,

I spring out of bed and decide
to roll up my life into a fist,
smelling of patchouli and roses, and then

unroll it; and to my surprise
it becomes a snail's yellow shell,
unravelling. On and on it goes,

I tap tap my red shoes,
find I'm already home.

Roshan

Three quarters of the way into my name,
there's Roshan, roshni, light; that seems to me right,

a silver of bangles on a wrist, round mirror chips
embroidered into the hem of my clothes,

my white skin seen tiny times over,
sequins sewn into my childhood.

This is my light; a cloth weighted
with five bright beads over an English lamp.

And me now, turning on these lights in the dusk,
move still with a shake of bells at my feet,

not quite heard, the light not quite seen.

My Mother Moves into Adolescence

My mother comes round with my star signs,
a thin apple pie, shop-bought that no-one will want
and the *Daily Mail*. I say thank you.

She presents me with six more things:

1.
You must sort out breakdown for my car Debbie
because my English is bad.
I get the leaflet, circle the right policy, hand it back to her.

2.
Where must I buy new front door?
B&Q? Homebase? I said that before, Mum.
She waits for me to offer to measure it and take her.
I put the kettle on.

3.
Where do I find man to fit new door?
I don't know, Mum, look in Yellow Pages?
She waits for me to get her the Yellow Pages.
I get her a piece of cake with her tea.
Just a thin piece… chorti… chorti.
She eats a large piece, noisily.

4.
Where do I find man to fit carpet?
Yellow Pages, Mum?
Where do I look under?
Carpet Fitters, Mum.

5.

You must show me where to write email to Aleem.
I show her.

6.

I need you write letter to estate agent.
I can't do it today, Mum.
You are so lazy Debbie! she screams.
All her rage spits out.
She throws her mug into the sink and it shatters there.

I liked that green mug with the spots,
from Woolworths.
There is no more Woolworths.
Suddenly,
terribly, unbearably sad
that there is no Woolworths,
I tell her to go and never come back.

Mustard Cardigan

My mother cannot kneel easily
in her silk sari, but she is beautiful
at the foot of my bed,
scarlet painted nails threading
the shiny buttons to fasten
my new mustard cardigan,

Deb-or-rah!
a call comes from the kitchen
plumb-round vowels, imperious,
I can do nothing but listen

and my Mother's bangles slip
along her thin arms,
as she hovers there, uncertain,
my buttons half-undone,

her little blonde doll,
not yet dressed,
makes her escape
and my mother
kneels to no-one.

In the heat of her kitchen,
my grandmother's *tsk* is loving
as she bends from her work,
shows me just how
to push the slippery buttons,

mother-of -pearl,
through small woolly holes.
My fingers fumble, the task is hard,
but I learn how to do it.

I choose this kind of love.

Naive City Eyes

I picked her up
on the way to see my boyfriend,
partly for company and partly
to show him how unexpected
I could be, to intrigue him.

She looked harmless, a hippy,
Greenpeace bag, naive city eyes.
It was rainy, she was grateful,
even though I could only take her
part of the way.

Sorry I have to call in and get my bloke from work,
I said. She didn't mind.
We got on really well; I could see me in her a bit,
twenty years ago, before babies, divorce,
Guardian Soulmates, other shit.

The trouble was my boyfriend,
a health and safety officer, today
working at the abbattoir in Rhyader,
getting into the car, stepping out
of the shiny red puddles,

smelling strongly of beef;
turning to smile at her,
blood splashes
on his white collar,
teeth.

I Don't Know Why

Only god or his grandmother
could love him the way he wants to be loved.
As for me love sits
fly and spider in my chest.
Not enough he says I must pay
pulls open wide lips slips
the bird, a small one, its breast
feathers forked tail
snapped over pushed down shoved
between teeth over tongue stuffed
swallowed warm as a lover.

After the bird the spider the fly
I got the idea, knew the score.
I accepted, ate more, loved less
wondered why I stayed.
I gave up hope and gentleness,
the pain became hard to ignore.
My ageing, my inertia was paid
in bitterness, after dinner chocolates,
a freezer full of cuts of the best.
I lie beside him sick of the mess.
Perhaps I'll die.

Still Life

Digby's approach is to sweep things under the carpet.
Sometimes he hoovers them up
but then he can't sleep
imagines them still alive

in the clear plastic cylinder
the ugly words
the cunts, the bastards, the bitches
that lay wriggling around her

that he threw
not imagining the mess. Next time
under the carpet. Definitely. Yes. Then
if there's still life there, he will not see

as he pulls the words from under her feet,
as he stamps and stamps and stamps.

Troll

Caradoc Coaches, day trip-*trap trip-trap*
over the bridge to Llanbister, to Lyn Gwynant,
bridges of devils and the coach *put-put*
it goes, so slow, slow as red kites
whooshing the wind to the water
to dip, like the road to elsewhere.

Where I might step from the green bus
and wander off past the shelter's red painted
Anwen Price is a Slut
to climb up past the peckled rocks there

and as the bus dreeps to the distance
take off my shoes to press my bare feet
my head to the sheep-bitten grass
so tight it is so pillow soft
and sleep.

Tŷ Duw

Into the house of the dead priest, I bring fresh air,
lift the blinds, turn on lights,

so as to imagine that there could ever be life here.
I flush the toilets, open the taps

water, red as blood stutters out.
A thick must, dust of ages settled

on velvet curtains, a hush of ecclesiastical oak,
an altar, seven golden candlesticks,

penitent chairs in rows,
and the book open at Revelation.

Into the house of the dead priest three neighbours come,
which is, and which was, and which is to come;

the last stands too close, his breath of onions,
his voice the sound of many waters,

but I see that the hair on his head and his beard are of snow,
that he has a reverent air of wanting to know,

if the clues are still fresh, if the priest was right,
if I hold the keys of hell and of death.

Cockle Wives at Penclawdd

The women of the Gower ride out on their donkeys,
bundled up round and rolling with the pony carts,
stretched out in a line, following the tide's edges.
They are going to gather the cockles
left on the shore by the ebb.

Theirs is a hard life, at times ten miles
to the cockle beds. They carry their rakes and sieves,
carry their boots laced around necks
to save the leather, carry their husband's names,
the Davis's and the Hughes of Penclawdd,
round as the rolling of the pony carts.

No shirking even on wintery mornings;
on the mud flats, they sieve all the small ones out
and leave them to grow on,
taking only the three year old cockle
with its rings like the rings of a tree.
They take care to lift their skirts,
squat to a piss, away from the cockles
with their little open mouths.

Sometimes twelve hundred women bundled round
picking the cockles on the beach. And then
they ride home on their donkeys, home to the men
rolling wider and rounder, sacks full to the brim;
with the cockles that click and clack

and mutter as they sway.

The Head of the Church in Rome

Since Saint Peter, the rock,
the cocks of the cardinals,
the penises of the popes
have been pickled and preserved,
cauterised and kept
with ancient unguents
and prayers.

Peter, rock of ages;
it floats, shepherded
amongst those pale others.

Pope Nicolas swollen and engorged
by the pickling process,
has sunk to the bottom,

bits of it flaking off
and floating
as scum on the surface.

Pope Leo the Great, tiny.
Pope Joan, missing,
Julius II, covered in sores.

Pontiff, patriarch, these keys
to the kingdom of heaven float;
open their tiny mouths,
sip the vinegar sour as sin.

When You're Ready, The Right Man Will Come Along

Taking my cup of tea back to bed this morning,
the air was still, but I could just see, obliquely,
the telegraph wire stretched across the street
vibrating and sagging quite alarmingly.

What bloody heavy sodding bird is that?
I wondered and just as I thought it
he came into view, a man all in green
and sparkling, legs all slim and toes
pointy, pole shaking, slinking along it,
shoulders broad and fine, strong thighs
pinging and stretching like the wire.

He caught my eye and grinned.
I nodded but didn't want to distract him,
so slid beneath the covers.
When I came up for air he had gone.

Later, coming back from the Co-Op
a carrier-bag-for-life full of regret and relief,
I found green sequins scattered in the street.

The Dog Knows its Mistress

for Jim

Lie across my feet
blue-black dog, warm them.

Bring me coffee in a small cup
and allow me these moments of complaint

where there is no need for complaint,
let my white shoulders sag a little

scratch my back where the bra strap
is too tight and release the clasp

let my breasts sag and sigh out
with a wonder of release

I shall stroke your ears in return
and for what we are about to repeat

may you be truly thankful.

You are the Blue-Black Dog

After the painting 'Under the Stars with Cats & Oranges'
by Gigi Mills

She sits with her dazzled face lifted skyways
her broad rump comfy on banks of lemon thyme
her arms around her big blue-black dog

that sits, licks at her life, her legs wide as the night,
a ruffle of soft grey frock and stars that sing
of no other time but this – and then a thin white cat

slinks in, lifts its velvet paw up as though
to catch the stars that fuzz the dark landscape
with cross-stitches of white, and the oranges,

three small fruits that hang and wait
for their own art to be peeled back and released.

Thighs

Once I could get the lids from difficult jars with my thighs,
cradle injured birds, wrestle attacking Picts with humour
and my thighs. Once a lover wrote his name, pressed
the still-firm skin with biro, drew arrows of desire;
I could drop grapes straight into his open mouth,
holding his head steady with just my thighs.
Now, in the evenings I rub butter
along them, looking for signs.
Oh we must face the horror
soon enough.

Getting It

To start with, I tried sex with a space hopper;
rolled it around in the corner of my bedroom,
whilst it smiled its dirty smile,
and looked like it might help,
but not, quite.

I tried sex with an old friend,
safe on the sofa; I felt something,
like tracing the lines
on my own palm, sweet dead ends.
Avoided him spending the night.

I tried safe-sex with soft-swingers,
rubbed against the Hitler moustaches
of middle-class women,
drank tea in the intermission
in a Llandrindod Wells hotel.

Alone now in my bed,
I hear a peal of bells, on and on, a joy in my head.
My search flies from hands
outstretched.

Splitting up in China with Bitterley Bear

Take some photos and take our bear,
Miss Price from Bitterley School
says to my children,

in photographs at Tiananmen Square
and the Forbidden City you can see
he does not belong there.

We four, and Bitterley Bear –
this embittered family.

Bear sleeps with his own dreams,
not touching anyone,
not anyone.

Home,
picking at fallen stitches,
the artificial stuffing,
I tear its eyes out.

Everywhere We Looked

This winter, in our forties,
chatting over the washing up,
my sister and I discovered
that she'd always coveted
the grey green eyes of my birth,
and I, hers of golden brown,
and *Don't It Make My Brown Eyes*
was never personal enough.

So we swapped, we popped out
our eyeballs, slipped them
into our mouths to moisten them,
before slotting into familial sockets,
left with little chance of rejection,
each looking into our own eyes.

I put a pen in my cunt once

I put a pen in my cunt once
just to play with myself
when I was at a loose end
when we were in one of those times
lying in straight lines in the dark
not touching

long hands stroke
my words to sour cream
this is what it wrote

Writing Poems

This country kid in my class
used to take down the soft pelts

from farmers' fences, cut off
their little heads and thread them

on strings to dry, then, with mother-of-pearl
tweezers and some fine silk, make zips

from the teeth, a long mole smile
he would stitch into mole skin pencil cases.

Sometimes, as a good luck charm,
there'd be a little dead mole head,

toothless, dangling. The heat in the classroom
that summer and the smell of the poems in pencil.

Chicken

I had a strange husband once.
Four years, long enough for it to hurt me badly,
so that I'd always be able to roll up my shirt,
have the scars to show.

We heal more slowly as we age,
don't quite recover our old selves,
falter at the edges of pavements,
not even sure anymore
that we want to cross the road.

Small Town

Twenty years in this town
where I brought up babies,
ate in the cafés,
worked on the till in Tesco's.

Now, I slip through its streets,
avoid eye contact. These days
I go to Aldi, even though the kids
won't eat the cereal.

Its aisles are empty. No Rose here,
or Tina with the belly laugh
and the dirty jokes
and the *so how's married life treating you?*

And although I know which steps
spring will take, daffodils,
some unexpected sun on a wet hillside,
Crème Eggs by the tills,
I no longer trust even this;

and it's something to do
with what you did to me.

Dissociation

Whenever he shouted at me
his spittle would fly out,
I would watch where it landed
with some fascination –

when in the kitchen, a mental note
to get out anti-bacterial spray
for after he had finished –
but he was remarkable,

he could go on for hours,
maybe sometimes I'd forget
and the kitchen
never felt quite clean after that.

I'd marvel at how fast and far
it could travel, often to fly
and land in a perfect parabola
across the dressing-table mirror

in our bedroom and I'd see
how the light would shine through it
like tiny pearls
strung along a woman's throat.

Sometimes, and often
it would fall on my face
but I did not feel that.

Fridge Magnets

Middle-aged women
who have had some pain in their lives,
are very wise. They kindly come over
with cakes and cards and fridge magnets
with wisdom written thereon:

A woman is like a teabag
Stronger in hot water

And now, my fridge magnet collection
covers the whole of the fridge.

The big wisdom, they say, the hard one, is:
You must live in the present
Launch Yourself On Every Wave,
Find Eternity In Every Moment.

Can't they see that I am?
I shout it so they can hear it.
I Don't Cry Because It's Over,
I Smile Because It Happened.

Now I am ready.

The friends shake their heads, wrap scarves over their hair
like widows at wakes, and leave.

Seeing It Coming

Francine started to use rear-view mirrors
for walking. To start with she bound
a *Halford's Basic,* round and round
with tape to her left arm, found
it made her arm ache, stopped the blood,
didn't go far enough on the right-hand side.

And so she tried convex, concave,
adjustable arms and Mini mirrors
stitched to her cardi, but they sagged
and all was distorted in the glass.
She saw only her arse, the grey pavement,
and the holes in the road.

Finally, late night blanket-stitch,
cross-stitch tight, she fastened
white van mirrors, angel's wings,
into the seams of her great-coat,
mounted on reinforced shoulder pads
so they wouldn't rub,
and then she could see whatever might come
from out of her blind spot.

Dirty Laundry

I sit with my hands clasped
in my fat lap
my back to the painting
I refuse the art
but take the cakes
I can't help it.

I wear your old grey dressing-gown
with its roll-up smell
to the bathroom in the morning
and coming back to you
let it part to show
my legs, my breasts
but you are either too polite
to watch my curves
or I am too old
and don't enchant you.

I recall the lust of other lovers
from your blank eyes
and go and empty the washing
from the machine
and go out into the garden
where there is certainty of rain.

Stretching up my arms
I let the grey gown part
and feel the morning chill
snake along my thighs
like desire, like
a young lover's gaze.

I hang up a rough white linen sheet
some pretty skirts,
a raspberry nightie
and lemon-yellow pants.

I am wiser than Canute
against a tide of grey.

Like Chocolate

1.
He has a loose thin body hidden in loose thin clothes
a passion for painting that I love
and I am addicted to him like chocolate.
Both are bad for me.

Charlotte says
        Leave it alone. He's not right for you.
Of course she knows me, she's right.

He loves art but for an artist he has no imagination
this makes him selfish.
I dance around him, silver,
a fish out of water, reeled in.

When we make love
he closes his eyes,
takes himself seriously.

He loves the sound of colours,
magenta ochre burnt umber,
a litany of names thick on his brush,
and says he is blue like the *blue of grape hyacinth,*
gentian, borage, the flax flower.

I wish he would speak my name so lovingly.

2.
        I think I'm pregnant.
I tell Charlotte, running my finger
through condensation on the kitchen window.
Charlotte lifts my hand from the glass,
turns it carefully over between her hands,
moves her finger across the lines on my palm.

I pull my hand away, I cannot bear the tenderness.

3.
I think that I might tell him,
as we walk through autumn woods,
but his words ricochet,
are lost in the big spaces
between the magenta and ochre trees.

4.
Sick sick in my stomach
I wait like a teenager by the phone.
Then in the night the dragging down blood comes.

I ring Charlotte.
She comes over to make me sweet tea
and cry.

I feel empty, empty but that is better.

5.
Two days later I am laughing with Charlotte,
we are moving a mattress downstairs,
moving mattresses always makes me laugh
and it is him at the door.
I slide down the wall, sit on the floor.

He has been to see his ex.
they had a terrible row and she hit him.
He has a cut above his left eye.
I bathe it with salt water. He winces.
        I'm sorry.

Charlotte sits in my kitchen.
        I never thought you could be so stupid.

6.

His cottage is small and cluttered.
Over warm
and stuffed with his jewel-like paintings.

She's agreed that I can stay for a while.
He is stacking frames into a box.
He leans over, looks me in the eye, kisses me on the
forehead.

7.

He'll be back. Charlotte says,
Sniffing round when she kicks him out again.

I seem to find some comfort in this.

List of blue flowers taken from *Werner's Nomenclature of
Colours* (1821).

The Angel in the House

She stifles a sneeze; from the dust, the dog,
the white feathers that scurry at edges
and the cold remains
of incense and another burnt dinner.
He is sensitive to noise.

He nods at her tea.
He says *Didn't you make me one?*
Sorry, she says.

She makes him some tea.

He goes back upstairs;
to writing his novel; *this* novel,
the third novel, is his great novel.
She thinks, *I'd better put another load on.*

She puts another load on.

Carrying so much weight,
she hangs up her wings
in the under-stairs cupboard.

She takes up the three-pronged fork

feels the nub and itch of the tail,
and the stubs of horns,
the white feathers, after all,
keep blocking the filter in the hoover

and making her sneeze.

In Sex We Sing

In sex we sing
strong as blackbirds,
as bird-feathered, tarred
and feather-brained
we nest on pillows, fight
over the wish-bone
as it splits.

New House

Strange, that house,
after years in another loved place,
where I could find its bones,
a warm pulse, blindfolded.

On the first warm days at the end
of that long winter, bull-frogs came
out of nowhere, found our pond
and sat fat and horny, singing.

I could not walk out in the dark,
for fear of treading their several leaf shades,
into the mud.

Now my dreams flood
with the desperation of frogs,
careless for lust.

Small Rain

I fall asleep easily these days.
The salt light shortens and lengthens, projects
especially shadows and I imagine myself

a 1950s baby, overwrapped in a perambulator
with its bouncing chassis, in an autumn garden,
a muffler, a plaid blanket, a shawl
of crochet squares of red and orange and brown.

A passing of clouds over the sun
sends a chill to fingertips, over-peeping the blanket,
grasping and curled. I imagine my 1950s mother,
breathing Craven A smoke through her nose,

red-tipped second finger taking the tobacco grain
from her tongue, feeling small rain and judging
just how damp from the slow flap of the washing
and the red apple-flush of sleep in my cheeks;

just how long.

Anwen & the Shark

In my house I have the Font of All Knowledge;
I found it at a car boot sale,
the man said it was working as far as he knew
and so I decided to take the risk.

I filled it with water, plugged it in
and a fountain sprinkled; there's a light switch,
three different colour settings
and it looks good at night.

I floated flowers, a plastic mermaid called Anwen
and a shark. One after another my friends
came round, cast plastic flowers to appease
troubled waters and many things were resolved.

I forgave you and moved on.
But knowledge isn't everything
and despite the wisdom,
it blew a fuse.

I took Anwen dripping from the water,
pulled off her head holding onto the Y
of her tail and her purple hair.
Topped and tailed, I inserted the pink nub
of her into the mouth of the shark.

And it was only then that I felt much better.

Heptonstall

A young man watches a girl
with crazy red hair and a yellow knitted hat
jump over the wall, wander erratic as the graves;
I can see in her body that she knows
she has him in thrall. This strange summer,
the graveyard, Heptonstall.

On a bench an elderly couple
sigh their rest there,
he looks into her face as she shades a glance
up to follow a buzzard's lazy screech and yaw.

We stand somewhere in between,
middle aged and still starting out
I do not risk moving off to test it,
the pull weaker than I have known.

I will shake off this man. I am wise enough,
witch enough to know that I can cast again.
The casting, the line fast at both ends.

'I can't put toothbrushes in a poem'

Sylvia Plath interviewed by Peter Orr, Oct 1962

Dearest darling deep voiced young faced Sylvia,
        of course you can do what you want,
        of course you can sing songs
of toothbrushes.

Don't you know therein lies your early-morning,
late-at-night salvation, in that particular grace.

Poets don't just need to feed on air –
root yourself in slow patience,
wiping sticky marks from a high chair;
the hurt and the fury must wait.

You must go to Boots and buy them;
soft and medium bristled,
pink and blue.

He Sees Me

I like this man who,
charmed by me,
slips alongside and inside of me
like the tongue of a dog
lapping at my life.

He says I rise up like a hundred balloons
loosed from a child's hand,
beautiful, bold, even when out of sight.

He says when I sleep I sigh
and he watches me wake and smiles
at the fuzz of my hair
and my mind in the morning.

He is charmed, he is charmed;
I begin to charm even myself
he sees me so lovely.

On Ageing

That a path runs through the house is not odd;
that it is a gravel path and is uncomfortably narrow
makes sense to me and I follow it, careful not to kick
the grey stones onto the floorboards;
it takes me down and out to a dark garden
where strings of white lights wrap twisted branches.

And here she is, the crone in her feathered nest,
white skin and naked, she cowers in the dark, pressed
hard against the thickly woven wood. She spits feathers.
She recovers herself and passes me a folded fan
of coloured cloth and I take it upstairs, to the room
filled with light, unravel its japanned panels,
a white lily, lavender, a dandelion, a rose.

But it is hers, and though I try to fold it,
to fold it to its neat shape, it will never go back.
I see her hover in the doorway,
Oh but I cannot make this neat again.
I cannot get it back to how it was before.

Deep Pockets

I sit in the kitchen
in a yellow-striped dress
with deep pockets

thrusting my hands deep,
there is string, a pin,
garden wire and three sweet-pea seeds.

I sit sullen like a child.

On the table a rough grey
plate with flecks of blue and four
chocolate dainty cakes
and five of us in this house.

Pink Pyjama Suit

I must have been just five,
in my pink, shiny shalwar kameez.

Auntie, Karachi, pinched my cheeks,
Chorti pyara, like a doll
like a little blonde doll.
Walk this way, try some dancing.
Behen! Now you have
your little blonde doll to play with!

Mummi-ji, I don't want to wear it to school.
North London laughs too easily,
makes fools of us and this mix-up family, this
half-caste council-estate bastard.

Miss Minchin, one arm shorter than the other
knew how North London could laugh, and said:
Knock on all six doors and tell them
Miss Minchin says I must show the children
my clothes from Pakistan.

Mummi-ji, the glass on the doors is too high
and all those eyes
as I turn round and round, up on teachers' tables
to twist in my pretty pink pyjama suit
like a little blonde doll.

Epping Forest

That great ancient picnic place where Londoners go to die,
to hang blotched and purple from a pollarded beech,
to stuff up the pipes of their Vauxhall Velux,
Cortina, or Fiat Supermiafiori, to drown in gunfire blue pools,
or to lie down in the stink of their own paracetamol-flavoured mess.

Robert Curly was a doctor and from his son,
we heard these stories of the woods just out of town,
how his dad would be called there to name them dead.

I forget how you were going to do it now,
I guess in some water, a deep forest pool,
although you could swim. The telephone box,
a light in the darkness, a red clearing in the trees,
with little woodland creatures' eyes watching
your snot and snivel, as you fumble for change,
unsteadied on the swing of Yellow Pages,

as you call me to save you.

Me just thirteen or fourteen, frightened,
talking you home.

No-one but the AA

Lonely is
on the last train,
winter,
the late late night train,
winter,
hot and buzzing as the train
waiting,
a red light behind the eyes,
mad with that dull
waiting.

Lonely is
a car crash in a country lane
in ice,
skidded wheels and slurred hedges
and ice,
and pumped heart is, as flat tyres
and silence
the night, as ice is
and no-one but the AA to call,
and silence.

Lonely is
a figure crossing a bridge on a day
of grey,
over moving traffic,
and grey
straight road lines
to London,
to life,
as if it was all over there,
all over there,
your life.

See here what lonely is,
it is standing still whilst others
have homes, beds, arms to slip into.

Lift Him Up Out

He was always drawn to this kind of woman,
the kind who would survive a nuclear exchange;

the kind who, he felt, would lift him up out
of the wreckage of the car crash by his cock

and his pinched nipples, his body arched up
and greedy for her mouth; the kind of woman

who, on his deathbed, would say something
to take his mind off it, to give him something

(even as the breath gave up)
to live for.

Playing Scrabble with my new lover

So stupid, but I hadn't remembered
that the last time I'd played
was in the old house,
until I found the four stubby pencils
and old scores, settled.

I poured the wine, apologised
for not being much fun,
while he spelt out LOVE;

But his score was only seven
and I said,
You should have kept the V
for another time.

The Magic Spell

Sewn into a tiny felt pocket, pinned into my knickers is my magic spell. A gift or curse, I cannot tell. The spell is this: if I ever speak to a man, look straight in his eye and he speaks right back, he falls in love with me.

Once at a publishing party on Vauxhall Bridge Road, talking to an actor from the film of the book; taller than I had imagined, much more beautiful, wearing a black woollen poncho, Levis, and slip on leather sandals, wide and long as boats on his feet. He was saying *Yes I have to get shoes specially made from a shop on Oxford Street*, when the spell overcame him. He struggled to compose himself, *There's something about you, have we met before?* Shaking his head, the tall Italian woman in a little black dress by the door opened her wide lip-sticked mouth, showed him her perfect teeth. He looked back down at my dull hair, my warm-for-the-weather cardi and sensible shoes. *I believe we may both be old souls,* earnest, intent, slightly distressed; like that bit in the film when he tries to save his woman from dying in a cave. He whispered about his long interest in reiki, the power of crystals, the importance of following your spiritual destiny, and would I come to tantric yoga? I opened my mouth to speak, despite his extreme beauty, the warm dry feel of his hand, I turned him down.

A man is always there for me, panting like a dog with love. The vet, the man in Homebase, the postman; friends, husbands of friends, the man who services my car. Plagued with requests for marriage and fidelity, they are shy, helpless and speechless, but I can see it in their eyes as it passes through them like wine through water.

I live alone. Keep chickens, ducks, no lovers. They are there for the spell and not for me. I do not believe in them.

Today on the train I sit and unpick the stitches that hold in my spell, turn it over and over in my fingers, cool and smooth, innocuous. I seal it into a brown envelope, pass to the girl with me on this long journey; duffle-coated bespectacled, shy of any notice. Open this envelope. Take what you find there.

Brown Clee Hill

When I die my ghost will come here
I said, laughing. It will walk slowly

up the long drive stopping to say,
here is the mountain ash I planted

come tall now, here are the fattest blackberries,
here the hazel and the best holly for berries.

The oak tree over my first dog that died here,
and a stone for a rabbit that the boys saved

from the claws of the cat. And see, the bees
make the laburnum sing still, some are caught

in my old watering can fallen on its side,
a sound of summer, amplified.

And a plastic soldier taking aim,
still kneeling steadfast in the dirt.

Trust

They don't sting when they're in flower,
his hand held out, in a gesture
of grasping the nettle.

I watched him hesitate
before his fingers closed
hard against the dusty leaves.

He was right.
I hadn't believed him
but he didn't flinch.

Like a child I reached out
to take it in my hand.
It has been stinging all night.

Scurvy Knaves

These men, these *men*
putting on their masks,
stepping out from Hope Bay,
Hut Point, Patience Camp,
Deception Island;
this litany of names,
this un-heroic age.

And I am reminded of that longest of winters
where the sun ached into the sea
for the last time
and it's what interests me, this

space, the absence of warmth and light
and how we might survive it still.

and his wife could eat no lean

and so she grew fat, drifted more slowly
down paths of blown over roses,

over-grown in a garden where
she grew cabbage-babies

that lived and died, putting the loveliest
in the deepest-double-dug bed

and waited for them to take root,
a mandrake child,

but it never did show,
just that child of his and its shadow,

its empty space filled by this cuckoo,
its open-mouthed gape, spit

and chick-wide mouth suckling there,
licking her clean;

and his wife could never grow a child,
and between them both

ranged only chick-weed and words,
hen-pecked, and birds she kept for eggs,

that rambled over and over
and through and through.

Fortune always has to cut a deal

Fortune lives in a hut
in the garden

gravel and lavender creep
up to meet the steps

the inside milk white
and the outside

to match the iron bench
and the sky is blue

it is to write poems in
to please Fortune

to tip my hat to her
I take a little teapot

with some smoky tea
and two china cups

laid out with a silver spoon
on an embroidered tray-cloth

I sit and sharpen two new pencils
and as luck would have it

the cat brings in
two unsettled leaves.

Little Blue Pot

When I am old, will I carry
a re-useable jute carrier bag
the same colour as my clothes?

Will I slip, stealth-like under
the radar of men who might have once
held my glance a little too long?

Will a lover recognise me
from more than 200 yards
across a car boot sale

where I have bought
a little blue pot for my pins?

She describes herself like this

I still choose the window seat on buses,
trains and planes and though for now
all I can see is my own reflection
in the glass, in the fading light,
sometimes I can see beyond it.

I am a mother, a field   a house.
Without me, windows darken,
no-one else knows how to put on lights
just to bring the house to life.

I am each of the processes of laundry,
but most, the unfolding in winter
of sheets –   a sudden punch
of trapped summer on white linen – heat.

I have had many lovers
and I have been many times loved.
When I come I cry out,

and I am the sound of the wind in the trees

and I am the rain on the roof when in love,

or falling.

Acknowledgments and Thanks

Acknowledgments are due to the Editors of the following publications where these poems, or earlier versions, first appeared:

'Flock' was first published as 'Melancholy' in *The Fat Damsel* (2017). 'He Sees Me' first published in *Hallelujah for 50ft Women* (Bloodaxe, 2015). 'I Don't Know Why' first published in *Under the Radar* (Nine Arches Press, 2012). 'I put a pen in my cunt once', was first published in *Hallelujah for 50ft Women* (Bloodaxe, 2015). 'My Brown-Eyed Girl', first published in *Wenlock Poetry Festival Anthology,* 2015 (Fair Acre Press). 'My Mother Moves into Adolescence' first published in *Motherhood* (The Emma Press, 2014). 'On Sleeping Alone', was first published on the website *Ink, Sweat and Tears* (2012). 'Playing Scrabble with my new lover' was first published in *Here Comes Everyone* (Silhouette Press, 2016). 'Roshan' was first published in *Light – A National Poetry Day Book,* edited by Gaby Morgan (2015). 'Then in June' was first published as 'Stronger and Fatter' by Sarah James as part of her 'With You in Mind' blog (2015).

Some of the poems first appeared in *True Tales of the Countryside* published by The Emma Press (2015).

I'd like to thank my editor Jane Commane for having faith in this work and for being such a lovely person; unfailingly positive and wise.

Thank you to the artist Gigi Mills for permission to use her lovely painting 'Nude with Poppies' for the cover.

I was really grateful for an opportunity to benefit from The Literary Consultancy Free Read scheme back when I was a low income, single parent and desperate for any encouragement. And to The Arvon Foundation for a funded place at The Hurst on a poetry writing retreat with the wonderful Jean Sprackland & Jacob Polley.

And of course thanks and love to James Sheard for the unfailing cup of tea first thing in the morning and for everything else.